Searchng for Signal

SEARCHING for SIGNAL

LORI CAYER

Clarise Foster, Editor

Cover design by Doowah Design.
Photo of Lori Cayer by Jodey Hudey.

This book was printed on Ancient Forest Friendly paper.
Printed and bound in Canada by Hignell Book Printing Inc.

We acknowledge the support of The Canada Council for the Arts and the Manitoba Arts Council for our publishing program.

Library and Archives Canada Cataloguing in Publication

Title: Searching for signal / Lori Cayer ; Clarise Foster, editor.
Names: Cayer, Lori, author. | Foster, Clarise, 1955– editor.
Description: A poem.
Identifiers: Canadiana 20210137002 | ISBN 9781773240916 (softcover)
Classification: LCC PS8605.A94 S43 2021 | DDC C811/.6–dc23

Signature Editions
P.O. Box 206, RPO Corydon, Winnipeg, Manitoba, R3M 3S7
www.signature-editions.com

In memory of my father
Verne Wesley Kachkowski
1937-2008

tragedy, ecstasy, doom, and so on
— *Mark Rothko*

now you are wondering

why

you were even

       here

          describing

the precisely tinctured

          colour of

   air

sound

of the world going on with

out you

      without some sort of god

now you are walking into it

hoping it will be like

walking into

       the world's body finally

now you see

the whole

      fractal

        formula

           despairing

               outward

           molecule

        to

     atom

we go

        the recurring string of us

preamble

        thanksgiving circa

happy family hike

           past the collapsing

                canopy of autumn

along some farmer's

          cobby field snowed

with white beans

dropped during harvest

you walk into the trees

           like a father

step crisply out with your message
sideways eyes

          say you're likely
pissing blood again
despite that defiled organ

               carried

        away like

            an air balloon

(likely)
(again)
I think in muted tones

            of bending

        clenching
gleaning for a meal

           what was shed here

your hands taught us

how to gut fish

proper sanding technique

your Saturday painting class

passed down on Sunday

little tubes of overwhelming

lined up like children

my oak tree quite good you'd said

but in the final red

moments

I pushed in lickable thick apples

each with a tiny white mark

representing light

what you know of nature

and how to make it

blueblack for water

repeated scrapings

greens

that many commas

delicately jabbed

tree trunks paperwhite

paperweight

with barklike marks

and above the horizon line's imperative

(birdwing)
(bluewhiteblue)

splayed

as far as the eye

what can you say?

          after you

               say

you're not sorry

for your obvious failures to believe

                    in the invisible

spraying

        varnish without a mask

burning

        painted wood in the campfire

filling

       the tent with insecticide

                    understanding this

                    is a matter of version control

what you will discuss

memories rough-hewn

from history books

your father's distant side

some no-country

region of depreciated edges

Ukraine reduced to a language

a pin lost in a drawing called Galicia

(patchwork)
(mapshape)

fenced by someone's war spoils

othered

in their wretched shoes

on the same blighted dirt as their ancestors

their attempt at destiny

a trick of cartography

Canadian government man sent over

door-knocking the hovels

his promise of food on the table

didn't mention: No Ukrainians Wanted

they landed like a punch

in the same weatherbelt

as eastern Europe

frozen about the shoulders

indivisible latitudinal frequency

their arc of sorrow

you were not

war's boy

being born between

not maimed

not immigrant nor church

you were not

even a colour

refugee

only of your own household

blue eyes handing themselves down

on stolen land

I am recalling your face
in that office
when
        the last
                word entered it
boundary
end
final
      by its blue blue eye
I am grating along
one wheel
           off the edge

this is the bent

branch indicating our direction

          abandoned winter

                      nest

brought to your sudden bedside

               so

we might replace

          your presence

          on the trail

this is

your daughter's wedding

                  a snowy wood

you

           barely able

broken back

        briefly standing

              for the pictures

all of us buzzing like so many

                the light that day

                greyly failing and crisp snow

this is the advent of our colony collapse

you taken to your bed

            shaving there for dinner

you remember your mother's memoir

her calligraphy of ragged ballpoint

began in a horse cart age six

(oversaturated sky)
(clouds a grey herd)

her father moving them

north up Lake Manitoba

postmaster cheesemaker

she recalled him handsome

friendly curving mustache

meanwhile Winnipeg

that booming dream undreamed

gorgeous map dilation of stone

waited sixty years to meet her

your vertebrae transliterated
three sugar butterflies

                crack

                crumble

                crush

on a dive boat in Mexico
seventy pounds of gear turtling your back

        meta   (beyond)

        stasis   (stillness)

now you are

(locked)

(down)

      the days keep falling

             dropped

morphine caps

         beneath your blue waiting-chair

we are doled out

one will finish your website

one your taxes

one those tables you made us

             ready for varnish

me

    the letters to the misdiagnosing

milk beads

on the carpet

your mother before her memoir

a sepia story of arising

from a blacksmith and a Fille du Roi

her pre-embodiment transmitted west

an ocean of water, another of dirt

their beacons long out of range

then on a frozen prairie your mother

begat by love

and without guile

her share of the sisters' trousseau:

> one tea set painted with birds
>
> in brown and rustic colours
>
> two milk cows from her father
>
> one set of flour sack sheets

before certain things in life surprised her

while you are waiting

                you issue

no

epiphanies

        no

           grasping-straws

but thank

        you

thank you

for sitting by

what else you will discuss

northern Saskatchewan

(boreal)
(bird-filled)

rail trestle bridge

A-frame legs of boys jumping

global-nothing back when

now your old Red Deer river gone dry

sad
stony
old
furrow

your youth moonscaped

no fit stowage for bones

your new body

                  quakes like fawn

pushes along

stainless steel wheeled

                        from your bird-coloured chair

                        explain

how to fix the sticky door

                     tell

the age of each deer

from our picture

                 window descriptions

we are drawn up buckets

                        dipping for miracles

                        down the well

we were just travelling

                        along when suddenly

we are never the same

we are isolated biological entities

walking on the verge

                      static breaking

at the limits

you were another guy once

married to our mother

your two pairs of hands

critically estranged

your one pair never enough

you were that husband

creeping home

once too often at midnight

her bitter actions a fury

yours

amnesiac

banging at the locked doors

(town)
(so small)

she sent you to live in the dirt cellar

for a while fetching her potatoes

was unsettling

your cot and raggedy blankets down there

you were that father

trenched

unspoken

buffering detonations

tornado word hurlings

this is pattern recognition

is gene pool

unsubmerged

what do you say?

                when I throw a wide net

of talking

        hoping to catch the scaled skin

        of something to hold

what do you think about?

             all day

now books

now movies

have lost their meaning

           nothing

                you say

                    hours of

              your silence

        non-reflective

your workshop

our common hub

maple lacquer black oak

smell of sawdust

timber propanol

terpenic

volatile compounds

(incense)
(root)

comfort

tinge of anxiety

smell of you

to this day

they say we mostly marry someone

circumstantially adjacent

your father's parents

sown in dead-eyed dirt

children of the same village

same boat scant years apart

same region of Manitoba

they'd have known each other either continent

loveless necessity

married on a glacial lakebed

(bristled)
(clay stripe)

down the hide of this province

you've never been so

                    detached

succumbed

            what will be will be and so on

where are the world's disappointments

                                    now?

all your attempts

                that once planed you transparent

salted you dry

your body remembers

its first incomplete death

whooping the hundred-day cough

she sweated you

opened the window

town doctor said

when the leaves come green again

the child will live or die

so she sent for the Indigenous doctor

his boiled mixture

cooled by her breath

and dipped mouthward

so beautiful you should have been a girl

while you are waiting you want

        last things

at Christmas I search
Winnipeg's North End butchers

        for headcheese

(no)
(it's good)

    if you know how it's made now
but you can't enjoy it

       all the pills a violation
       your refusing throat

your mother

your dear sweet

ninety pounds of pin curls and scarf

toughest hen for miles

survival expert

of potatoes and dill

old coats sewn into quilts

hardscrabble love

of that particular man

dead of hard living at fifty-four

lucky for you all if you're honest

your window of probability

                     closing

you say you'd like to

                 maybe in the summer

prognosis drying up

like jerky on a branch

               maybe try for spring

you ask

did you write the letters?

                the snow

has begun to melt

I am made knowledgably kind

                        but unnecessary

by what I have learned

about your body

                its voiceless new language

of cause and effect

                mutagen and mutation

I am replacing you

                      in my own words

the feeling is

gravel

        shredded dermis

no bike

my list of topics incomplete

you were always fighting sadness

like a guy made of dough or clay

trapped in there

(thrum)
(headed)

looking for ways to interrupt misfortune

the windowed mail

at your workshop

unopened

taxation letters

sledding down your desk

that one Christmas you got a pillow

not posh but flat the way you like a pillow

how you doubled over punching it down

the joy of it

splitting you open

a moment

I am using up my allotted six years
of dreams

        always

                airports
                parking garages
                hotels

last night

        an exotic blue bird lifting off

or no

just the blue jays

           taking their morning meetings

blueing and jaying

           behind your house

you remember the time she fell

your mother from sunlight

from her beloved list of birds

sat for months

(this chair)
(or that)

something blind and aghast

had pulled the plug

at forty finally a girl

crying in the near distance

her little siren unheard

fed and rocked by the eldest

the father a barn door closed

until

neighbour lady stopped cheerfully by

saw the limp glove of her

shouted at the husband

packed her like a warm loaf

to hospital

while you are waiting

                          you call up
funeral homes

choose

          who is least expensive

choose

who is nicest on the phone

you were the first

high school enlightened

first journeyman

book reader

existential lightning rod

you may have begun

to wonder

how longitude

your ancestors meteor-dropped further south

might have changed anything

your new wife

holding your cold dinners

holding her tongue

you late for not getting a deer

late

for getting one

heavy as hell

for one guy in the mud to fold

into the car trunk

what you know of wood

multifarious steps toward

an entire building

set of kitchen cabinets

walnut and glass table for your mother

not till your sixties did you lose

three fingertips

mitre cut

bloodjumping

crickets

across the room

your father

with two strikes then three

a lifetime

temporary jobs

to make the smallest dollar

sucked from his pockets by booze

no one to pity him his luck

his demon

his battering ram mother

all he ever wanted

reliable work

a quiet wife

unhungry children

and enough for the demon

marching his blood

all the ways you're not

your father

you worked where you lived

everyone around

the table

your only devotion

you the nice parent

of the pair dealt us

you didn't drink your pay

come home a thousand times

with nothing but

enough gas in the truck to leave again

you have the right idea

        to love each geography

like a first-born

        add its nano-particles to your own

you send us out

        your prescription for joy

prairie forest mountains

then to the sea

flippered feet and glassed eyes

        to feel your reverence

in that third world

of under

I'm scanning the data bank of your enterprises

lifetime of diminishing investments

houses split up into rentals

restaurant owner

building inspector

sudden earthworm farm in the basement

etc. and that quaint anecdote

passing by Lynn Lake on a hunting trip

repossessed house bought on your card for nine hundred dollars

twelve-hour drive one way to be landlord

the gambler's paradox had you blind to folly

hereditary

thistle-rooted

to the suspect examples of the dead

we were never

        your good children

our relative lapses

        some going on under your very

        sleeping eyes

we make our mistakes

        like factory work

repeating what we don't know

        came before

you haven't been out
(out)
(doing)
out being
                your bluesky self
instead blanket-sitting
                        in this see-saw chair
there went winter's dry skis leaning
like two planks giving up on the job
                                spring's fishing rods
your shirts taken in
as your
timbers go
            scarecrow
a pressed and presentable sorrow

you were dirty thirties hunger

post depression-era hunger

world going on without your knowledge

wars, cities raising their tall buildings

the third generation

still living like pioneers

when you all built

your father's first real house

he already had cancer

(un)
(beknownst)

oldest boys ready to leave

you were a pulled bowstring

cans of evaporated milk

double punched

downed in a solid sluice

house left unpainted

a grim shade of mirage

driftwood

(ash)
(dustbowl)

your father worked home now

sawmill and farmland by seasons

but the rail pulsed a signal

its spindly arm

a vein through the trees

three times a week

off to town on the 5 o'clock

boat-staggering mean

on the midnight

you are that guy

whose last civic act

bed to wheelchair

is to vote against

Indigenous casino in city limits

you and me

each to our own

(petrified)
(etymologies)

same guy

with those same friends in the north

grew up with

net-fished with

hunted with

guy who doesn't answer for

your duplicities

who feeds

these deer

in your backyard

but hunts others to delicious sausage

admit

I do know this guy

you choose hospital

                  for this to happen

(this)

(cloak)

       of palliation

what was on the body at the time

of arrival fits

           in a prisoner's envelope

this is two metabolisms

each fighting

over the scraps of your life

your girls an accretion

    a range

        of antennas in need of

            hum

your boy pinging his sonar

           one foot near the door

I am taking up a collection

           of places you've been with guns

I am

    qualifying

        quantifying

           how

      you look

in your suit of bones

all the ways you are your father

schooled unknowingly

by his unsound work ethic

couldn't stand a boss

better for you

he was gone seeding

one man's farm every spring

harvesting another's in fall

felling trees further north over winter

ninety-five dollars per boxcar

because home

he was a leg-trapped badger

the mask fits imperfectly

your ideal future

dandled you

always jigging

just ahead

if you were judged by your worst day

who would you be?

certainly not repentant

another attempt is another chance

this time for the winner

between hospital-sleepings

                    you oversee

noisy builders upstairs

               constructing

               your next place

your fingers pick at

the blanket

count out the nails

                  suddenly closer to never

                I ask it

ask

if you know where you're going

(*yes*)

(you say)

in the language of most

                     certainly

your blue eye seeing it

                    but they told you

standing at the foot of your bed

your aunt

        your mother

        in that jade green blouse

        they told you not to say

so you do not say

               what stands

between now

and when

I send a message in moth-hovering
code
       to remember forever etc.
this downing light
              the long division of it
this shedding
         of waters
                and sediments
I read aloud a story about wild cats in the suburbs
you're listening
behind impossible
eyelids
       love dying of exposure

one day you rise up

        surprised

for a last taste of soup and a chat

your next place built

        our cream of potato time

                before

when next you wake

you will be outside

        a rapture of thwarted garden

still sprouting raspberries

the sun dragging its bright eyelid

           across the picture

your body remembers your father's death

doctor far too late

hospital refused

you next door with wife and babies

assigned every four hours

(night)
(day)

drive him to town for morphine

no longer shot glass but vial

glinting syringe silver

slippage into skin

some kind of war-ending injection

conquer the bull of him

for a few diminishing hours

you needing to

be a carpenter in the morning

lucky for us

your mother

our dear sweet

had two more lives after

one kindly marriage to a German widower

their main argument

if cabbage rolls should have meat

one lonesome old-person's apartment

her calligraphy before and after

no matter what he did

I will love that man till the day I die

if loneliness could be the perfect companion

long night drive

of a love like that

a giddy joy amongst us
instead of wail or wait
we crow-crowd

               around your breathing-bed
wingbeat

       liftings

           and touchings down
it is how we do this

          laughter
ringing from your room

             at the end
of the hall

this is your breath

                     packing up to go

your wild topographies

reduced

to square feet and milligrams

this has a scent

                  you smell like newborn baby

this is the most peaceful

(you have)

(ever)

nurse says

sometimes

        they want to do it alone

go home

(wait)

(while)

      the phone an hour later

butterfly taped to your door

       flew

something   from here

your white paper bonebox picked up

swaddled

      soothing velveteen bag

      same jay blue

of your eyes

(eye)

(blue)

neighbour sees us bring

you

    all in one pair of hands

he liked you

his car yanks too close

        to the edge

put you in your own toolbox

                       where better than

hardwood built true

              by your nineteen-year-old

journeyman hands

you didn't say

       after all

            where

    to go last

your first summer dead

                    does not happen for us either

                    though we perform

                    the camping ritual

listen for the waveshape

of your message

(sine   (sine   (sine

    sine)   sine)   sine)

                    look at each other

                    through the fidgeting arms

                    of campfire

we burn it day and night

the weather anon

your boats
          fishing gear
skis
    your scuba gear sold
your guns and tools absorbed into our houses
your ancient homemade wine declined
(chokecherry)
(rhubarb)
        we try out laughing
wish aloud we'd brought you
                along
gravelled in your toolbox
             save you
a lawn chair by the fire

while you were unreachable

a black exodus flowed

                          through the campsite

between chair legs and firepit

                               our lifted feet

black river of new ant colony moving house

multitude of egg sacs carried

                              you would have wanted

to see it

          their luggage of spilled rice

your canoe launch is where

        come fall

        with your bones decided

this gratitude spot easily found by satellite

(birch-voiced)

(uttered)

    what survives the kiln

     is transformed

from dirt to glass

your gathered rabble

       of broken cup

       ground-up pieces

and unglueable sand

each our fair share

          spilled

(slow)

(shallow)

 turn

     of creek

are we all so white inside?

              an envelope sent

this sun-warm

        this yellow and brown

this autumn

        still still green

your jay spears

        through our ministry

stating your name

                searching

                    for signal

what you knew of our houses

their bones and pipes

their dressings

you the guy we called

colours you made for my walls

(burnt nutmeg)
(north-facing lichen)

redwing for my office

adding black to raspberry

just enough

that it hurt to pour

as of this writing

             we all have kitchens

                          you haven't seen

wives husbands kids

on whom we place

              a hollow mark

                         we wish you could have

we are

petting each other's hands dry

in the telling

        if safe ends at you

        then we are terminal

if we are your exact same children

                (then safe)

                (is never)

sugar coated

        but still

chokecherry rhubarb when you bite down

what you knew of the forest

your private solace

your other job

rabbit
deer
moose

upwards of every edible bird and fish

prevailing drive to provide

what you knew of the forest

is what you knew of wood

its raw

       material

              concentric

       maker

of your days

your body remembers the marbles

you used as a calendar

each a contemplation

an appreciation for the day

you'd been given

then tossed

the jar emptying over years

you bought twenty years too many

we take them in our pockets

where we go

leave deposits of you

in the celluloid narrative

in the Bay of Pigs I launched

a blue-eyed one

in the glare

it fell into the sky twice

the sky

        should have

                but didn't

fall in after you

Acknowledgements

Some of the lines from these poems were published in a different format in *Prairie Fire Magazine*. Warm thanks to the team at Signature Editions: Karen Haughian, Ashley Brekelmans, Heidi Harms and to my editor Clarise Foster for her deft and articulate perspective. I am grateful to Maurice Meirau for his input on an early version of this manuscript and to Claire Ogden, Melanie Slavitch, Marlene Rumenovich and Dorene Willerton for historical and ancestral insights. A debt of thanks to Warren Cariou for a meaningful discussion of issues.

This book would not have been possible without the enduring presence of my family; my warmest thanks for their assistance offered by way of our collective memory. Lastly, I thank Todd Besant, my collaborator in life for his creative wisdom and long support.

Author's Note

Researching and writing this book was inevitably foregrounded by the ongoing discussions and questions of being a white settler writer whose forebears lived alongside, though never quite together with, Indigenous Peoples in the near north of Manitoba and Saskatchewan.

My earliest known forebear, a blacksmith called Antoine Caillé dit Brûlefer & Biscornet, emigrated from France in the late 1600s to what was labelled "New France." Although he is not listed as one of the known French Carignan soldiers sent to colonize the area, he nevertheless settled in the traditional territory of the Kanien'kehà:ka. He married Anne Aubry, a Filles du roi (King's Daughter), one of over 700 young French women delivered by King Louis XIV of France to marry the single Frenchmen that preceded them.

My Ukrainian ancestors were enticed to Canada in a settlement drive in the late 1800s, both sides settling on the lands and waters covered by Treaties 1, 2, 4, 5 and 6, the traditional territories of the Anishinaabeg, Cree, Oji-Cree, Dakota, and Dene Peoples, and the homeland of the Métis Nation.

I am grateful for the opportunity to write *Searching for Signal*—and my previous books—on Turtle Island, on the land and waters covered by Treaty 1. I hope it does justice to the story of my father's upbringing, without further entrenching and/or contributing to colonialist and settler attitudes and actions that brought much tragedy to, and continue to harm, Indigenous Peoples' families, Indigenous individuals and communities, and First Nations.

—Lori Cayer

About the Author

Lori Cayer is the author of four previous books of poetry, *Mrs Romanov*, which was shortlisted for the Lansdowne Prize for Poetry/ Prix Lansdowne de poésie, *Dopamine Blunder*, *Attenuations of Force*, also shortlisted for the Lansdowne Prize for Poetry/Prix Lansdowne de poésie, and *Stealing Mercury*, which was shortlisted for the McNally Robinson Book of the Year Award and won the Eileen McTavish Sykes Award for Best First Book in Manitoba. Lori is also a past winner of the John Hirsch Award for Most Promising Manitoba Writer. She is co-founder of the Lansdowne Prize for Poetry/Prix Lansdowne de poésie, Lori has lived her whole life on the now verdant bed of a glacial lake.

Eco-Audit
Printing this book using Rolland Enviro100 Book
instead of virgin fibres paper saved the following resources:

Trees	Electricity	Water	Air Emissions
2	3 GJ	1 m³	110 kg